Copywriting For Beginners:

Copywriting Secrets Guide to Writing a Successful Copy That Sells

By

Dale Blake

Table of Contents

Introduction 5

Chapter 1. Copywriting and Its Industry 6

Chapter 2. Being a Copywriter 7

Chapter 3. Benefits of Being a Copywriter 9

Chapter 4. Qualities of a Successful Copywriter 12

Chapter 5. Structure and Style 15

    The Headlines 15

    Qualities of a Good Headline 18

    Creating Powerful Contents 20

Chapter 5. Different Types of Copywriting 25

Chapter 6. Search Engine Optimization 28

Chapter 7. Perfecting The Output 30

Conclusion 32

Thank You Page 33

Copywriting For Beginners: Copywriting Secrets Guide to Writing a Successful Copy That Sells

By Dale Blake

© Copyright 2015 Dale Blake

Reproduction or translation of any part of this work beyond that permitted by section 107 or 108 of the 1976 United States Copyright Act without permission of the copyright owner is unlawful. Requests for permission or further information should be addressed to the author.

This publication is designed to provide accurate and authoritative information in regard to the subject matter covered. This work is sold with the understanding that the publisher is not engaged in rendering legal, accounting, or other professional services. If legal advice or other expert assistance is required, the services of a competent professional person should be sought.

First Published, 2015

Printed in the United States of America

Introduction

Various industries in marketing and sales are growing at exponential rates. After the discovery of the internet, not only the demands for top-notch copywriting service increased, but the process of hiring and employing them became much more simple. Thus, copywriting is now one of the most lucrative businesses and is a viable career option.

Although it is not a get-rich-overnight program, it is a sustainable source of income. With skills acquired through experience, a copywriter's value eventually increases along with his pay.

The industry of copywriting and the advantages of being a copywriter are detailed throughout this book. Furthermore, this book is created to effectively prepare you for the great ocean of opportunities in copywriting and succeed without fail.

Chapter 1. Copywriting and Its Industry

Almost anything, nowadays, can be marketed—goods, real estate properties, raw materials, the Internet and mobile phone connections, technological products and even talents and skills can be sold. In birth of the Internet has diversified the connections between various providers and clients. This rapid rate of consumerism gave birth to a new form of writing that is tailored for advertising and marketing: copywriting.

The primary objective of copywriting is to maximize sales and improve the popularity of a marketable object, property or service by persuasion. The words and phrase used for this type of writing is carefully selected and combined in such a way to influence the decisions of clients, buyers and readers. This is done by identifying the positive attributes of something that is desired to be marketed and highlighting them through a write up designed to make the target readers see how they would benefit from those.

Chapter 2. Being a Copywriter

Who are qualified to be copywriters?

Surprisingly, anyone can be a copywriter, provided that he has the necessary skills in writing and has a competent command over the language used. A degree is not necessary but having one is an advantage, particularly that on marketing and journalism as it will provide you with knowledge, concepts and needed experience to be a great one. Furthermore, although writing experience is beneficial as it sharpens ones writing prowess, it, too, is not necessary. What you need is a propensity for writing (something a person is born with or acquired through study and training), an excellent command over the language, attention or details and some creativity. Overtime, an experience sharpens one's ability.

Copywriters are among the highest paid writers around the world because of their direct influence on something that produces or generates money. On average, junior writers earn as much as $27,000-$33,000 a year while those who have gained experience through the field receive $70,000-$110,000 dollars or more.

Freelance Copywriting

A new form of copywriting, which takes advantage of the Internet, is gradually finding a significant space in the market. Freelance copywriters "write to order" articles and are paid either per article or per word. Common article orders are for web pages, sales brochures, press releases, trade magazines or for corporate video or flash presentations.

Chapter 3. Benefits of Being a Copywriter

Although there are many hypes circulating about freelance copywriting being a get-rich-quick solution, it is very similar to other forms of occupation with just the following benefits:

You get to call yourself a writer. You can brag around town or in social media saying you take your living from writing, and that would be a good thing to say and definitely bolster your self-confidence. Saying you are a writer gives your audience the impression that somehow you are similar with Shakespeare, Mark Twain or any other great writers who built their reputation through their abilities to command written words.

Flexibility of time and the freedom of choice. You get to choose your rate per hour of work or per word finished. You can even work on the times of the day where you are convenient. Conventional copywriters do not enjoy these benefits. However, copywriting is a serious and demanding job and needs to be given priority. You may think that copywriters are usually relaxed and free from stress or strain but the fact is, they are just more convenient but the level of hard work required is the same.

You work at the comfort of your homes. With freelance copywriting, you get to work right beside your family. You do not have to bother waking up early, prepare your clothes for work or drive a distance to work. You get to have quality time with your family while earning at the same time.

You learn. Before a copywriter, freelance or not, can write, he must first have something inside his head to write about. Copywriting is not about expressing your opinions or your self-serving emotions (which is easy, by the way) but about being direct to the point, factual and convincing. In order to be that, a copyreader must read and research always.

Copywriting for the Web

The web is a competitive environment for copywriters and copywriting for it is way different and difficult.

With the number of resources available, you can expect your readers to be very choosy. To be able to catch their attention, a write up needs to be interesting and engaging right from the start. Another thing to consider is search result placement. You may produce a well-written article but without following a necessary set of optimization protocols, it might end up at the end of the results page. Ranking high in a search engine result is necessary since most people only expect to find what they are looking for at the first three results that appear. In order to ensure a high rank in search engine results, a copywriter needs to employ a technique called [organic] *Search Engine Optimization* (SEO) techniques.

Chapter 4. Qualities of a Successful Copywriter

People become writers because they have a certain set of qualities born of them and a propensity for the discipline. Writers become copywriters because they follow certain rules and steps that enable them to develop qualities they could use to be more successful as the years unfold. The following list of qualities is not the attributes a writer must be born with but rather qualities that a writer must develop in himself to become a successful copywriter.

Ability to organize information. Articles required of copywriters are convincing. In order to be persuasive, it must be based on facts and should carefully point out beneficial details in order to bolster the reputation and image of the product or service they are writing for. Furthermore, he should be able to present those facts in an order that gradually convinces the readers of the importance of the product and how its features could benefit them. This ability is highly acquired and is developed over months or years of continued practice.

Clarity in presenting the advantages of the products. Copywriters are direct to the point and are focused. Unlike other writers for which the appeal of their write up *can be* derived from the degree of complexity of their metaphors and verbal calisthenics, the appeal of articles written by copywriters comes from the clarity of the presentation of the idea and the simplicity of the language used. They are also able to pinpoint the good qualities of a product a short glance. They are adept at sensing what the customer needs and meeting those with what the products could offer.

Mastery in refining ideas and concepts. A copywriter can only acquire through months or years of dedicated attention on details. The most successful copywriters are those able to explore ideas and concept and delved into them deeper in order to extract from them only the essence. Although few people are born with the aptitude to see ideas and concepts in their best angles, most people will take more mistakes first before they learn how to truly craft an idea into something worthwhile.

Creative commands of language. Not the use of jargon or highly confusing sentences or words—those are for thespians. Copywriters, on the other hand, are focused on creating convincing metaphors designed to make the readers imagine how it is like to experience the product. The metaphors they create can produce visuals that are capable of causing the feeling of satisfaction in the minds of the readers before they could even experience the using the product.

The qualities of a successful copywriter presented above do not aim to present qualities that an aspiring copywriter should have to dissuade them. They are presented in order to inform them of what attributes they need to develop and nurture within themselves as they gain experience in the field for a more fruitful career in copywriting in the future.

Chapter 5. Structure and Style

Persuasion is a difficult task—without the proper structure and tools, a human mind is difficult to convince since it will knowingly resist being altered of its idea. With the right techniques, however, a mind is easily swayed. Think about how long people of the past were convinced that the earth is flat or that the earth is the center of the Universe no matter how ridiculous they are to us today. They were ignorant and they were presented with something that both cure them of their ignorance and provide them amusement. Later on, when the earth was found to be round and that the planets moved around the Sun, people were not easily convinced by it. They needed proof before they did.

Similarly, in writing, what constitutes a structure that convinces? What style changes minds?

The Headlines

The first element of your write-up that your readers will notice is your headline. The quality of your headline will determine whether your article will be read or not. Studies reveal that 80 percent of readers will read your headline but only 20 percent actually read the content.

With so many competing elements for a person's attention, the only thing you would want to experience is have your readers read sentence after sentence in your article.

Here are some tips for writing compelling headlines:

Write the headlines first. It may sound absurd but some writers actually start their contents before deciding for a headline, which is also a valid writing technique, provided that they are not copywriting. In copywriting, you want your contents to be guided carefully to achieve a goal, and that goal can be defined early on with a headline.

Be inspired. Even freelance copywriting needs not mean a solitary life confined to a single space. Compile or collect winning sales letters, magazines or space ads. You can find an inspiration to these and a number more of resources that you can find either in the shelves and magazine racks of a bookstore or in the internet. Familiar yourself with how they are phrased, how the contents are connected to them and how they appeal to readers such as you.

Put keywords in the title. For copywriting intended for web, one of the most important aspects, perhaps equally important as the article itself, are the keywords used for *Search Engine Optimization*. The better optimized an article is for search engines, the higher it will rank in the results page. One way to ensure that is to include keywords in the posts or article title.

Qualities of a Good Headline

You may wonder why some headlines are so convincing; they usually compel readers to do a purchase while some do not. The reason is headlines need to meet certain qualities in order catch the attention of readers. Here is the list of qualities every headline must possess:

They give compelling and irresistible promise. A good headline gives a promise of a solution to a reader's problem. Most readers have already something in their minds when they are looking for something. The first headline that they see that matches this attracts their attention. Furthermore, the promise in the headline needs to be backed with answers and supporting statements in the article that is based from facts and truth. You do not want to lure in the first batch of buyers and stop there. You want them to access the product you are marketing and either creates another purchase or they recommend the product to others or both.

They are based from proven work. Newton said he saw further because he stood at the hands of the giants. You could receive an astounding and effective headline by creating one that is based on the effective and winning headlines of the past.

They are not a cheap copy of another. Although they are based from other headlines, they are not a copy of them. They are original with concepts taken from another and refined to give a better appeal.

Creating Powerful Contents

Next to an effectively engaging headline is the body. Just as a powerful headline convinces the readers to read, the content of the write up, an engaging content could establish the reputation of your product and finalize the persuasion.

Here are some tips to follow to create a powerfully persuasive body:

Narrate a story. Stories are effective because readers can relate to them. You can appeal to their visualization prowess by providing scenarios and situation involving the many ways that they can benefit to a product. Remember that a good copy encourages the readers to imagine themselves using and enjoying the product long before they actually use it.

Be conversational. You do not need to be formal and stiff with your language as with books. Unlike other forms of writing, copywriting takes its effects on interacting with the readers in the *human* level. Copywriting aims at providing contents that appeal to the person in the readers—something the readers can relate to—rather than be like an unfeeling and an insensitive robot. Use simple language and be direct to the point. Use the right word to describe what you want to convey.

Be Optimistic. Nobody likes misery. The more you allow your readers to see the bad side of your product the more you make them uncomfortable, which equates to zero sales and zero readership. Optimism, on the other hand, breeds interest. People are drawn to it because it gives them hope and assurance.

Repeat. Repeat. Repeat. Repetition reinforces memory and stores a word you repeat to the unconscious mind of the reader influencing his decisions later on. Perform repetition on key words. If possible, repeat keywords 3-4 times. The more you repeat the same word, the more they will be picked up by the readers' eyes and be brought into the brain where the neurons responsible for the memory of it get reinforced.

Use Figures and Facts. Nothing beats an article that is founded on truth backed by numbers taken from researches and data. Putting these on your copy makes it more reliable and trustworthy thus building your reputation as a copywriter. You can always state your claims whenever you write about a product but always back them up with evidence and testimonies. These will bolster that effect of your write-up on the readers.

Be organized in the presentation of facts. This tip is not only applicable to copywriters but to all types of writers, as well. Generally, in any form or writing, in order to maximize comprehension and to avoid misinterpretations, organizing data is necessary. Organizing data makes it easier to spot important aspects of the article. A cluttered data presentation does not only confuse readers but it disinterests them as well.

Avoid lengthy sentences and paragraphs. Copywriting is one of those fields in which giving so much does not guarantee receiving something much, too, in return. Sentences that are cluttered and has two or more complex sentences in a sentence, ruins the point or dulls its presence. Lengthy paragraphs are also disinteresting to readers. If possible and whenever possible, be brief, concise and be direct to the point.

Be simple. Write a copy as if they will be read by someone without a dictionary on hand. Besides, you do not need to impress the readers. Although that is needed, remember that the primary goal is to convince the readers more than to impress them. Simplicity is beauty, as the old saying goes.

Ask questions with "yes" answers. Asking a question with the yes answer makes the reader receptive to further suggestions. Ask them with simple questions first about anything they would agree. Gradually, write an article that leads into the question that you would really like to ask. You will be surprised at how people tend to be in favor of you after that.

Present the advantages of using a product to the readers. Readers may have probably stumbled in your article because they are looking for something. They may look for the product reviews or description but the truth is, they are looking for reasons on how it would benefit them.

Use the words *proven, free, now and unlimited*. They increase attention and readership by giving an image of lasting benefits. These words are meant to make the readers believe that something is exclusive or urgent. However, remember to use only those words to provide promises or claims that your product or service can fulfill. Do not say *free* when it is not or *unlimited* when its functions are limited in reality.

Appeal to Emotions. Emotions are more powerful than logical thinking because they are deeply rooted to what makes up our psyche. People do not decide based from facts (often) and from their logical reasoning but rather on emotions. We are all slaves to this neural chemical process. Thus, in order to write an effective copy, one must appeal to the emotions. Although emotions are difficult to predict and understand, they always serve as a guiding principle for choosing things.

Chapter 5. Different Types of Copywriting

The variety of industries necessitates different types of copywriting. Here are them:

SEO Copywriting. This type of writing is dedicated to producing articles that scores high on search engine results page--an important technique to reach a number of people at a short time. This type of writing follows the concept of keyword density in which a certain word will be repeated for a set number of times in the article in order to score high on SEO.

Sales copywriting. This type of writing requires a lot of creativity and a fine ability to persuade. This type of field requires a writing style aimed at persuading people to patronize a certain product.

Technical copywriting. In order for a writer to write for it, one must have an extensive and detailed knowledge about a certain product. This type of copywriting is probably one of the most difficult in the market today as it requires a particular degree of expertise

Content Copywriting. In this field, copywriters are only allowed to focus on one topic. Because of this, they write up could be as detailed and exhaustive as it needs to be.

Creative Copywriting. As artistry is usually a second nature to writing, this type of writing is most preferred by most writers, as it is one of the many avenues in which they can take advantage of their powerful imagination.

List of Copywriting Styles

Narrating. Most readers can relate to stories regardless of whether they are true or not. It takes and resembles the forms of a narrative account of something that has or has not been.

Down Home Copy. This type of copywriting creates the feeling to the readers as if the writer is talking to them. In this, the readers are the primary concern.

The you-copy. Although at some frequencies it may not always work, at times, creating articles that are centered on the readers do the trick. In order to do this, the writer thinks of a concept to deliver the message and add as many "you" as possible.

Shout copy. The sentences produced in this style have a characteristic of having many exclamation points providing the impression of shouting (sometimes labeled to by others as spamming.

Chapter 6. Search Engine Optimization

The purchasing behavior of people has undergone major changes since the discovery of the Internet. Before, people need to go to physical stores and select products. Today, whenever they want something, they just type in the words that match their concept to any search engines such as Yahoo!, Google, and Bing.

The usual scene is, once we type the words, result appear. This is where SEO must enter. SEO ensures that the article gets the highest position in the search engine results as possible. SEO ensures that you get the highest spot, or you get its equivalent.

Here are some tips on SEO:

Prioritize content length. Not only are longer contents more likely to get more links, a study also revealed that pages that are on top ranks have more than 2,000 words in them.

Think like a user/reader. Before thinking about what keywords to write, think of words to type in search engine to get to the site you have written for should you be the customer. You ca use the Google Keyword tool to assess what keywords users use.

Use long-trail keywords. This simply means to use long keywords. Long keywords are found to make a website or a copy rank higher in Google.

Include keywords in your topic title and optimize them afterwards. Ensure to make the title as natural as possible without removing the keywords

Chapter 7. Perfecting The Output

Successful writers, both copywriters and plain writers, adhere to the principles of high quality and standards. They do not write or submit a copy to clients without first finalizing the product to identify errors in grammar, syntax and contents. A minor slip either in grammar or in spelling, when noticed. Here are some tips to ensure all those are covered:

Print and proof it. This will enable you to catch errors and problems more. Unless you are born accustomed to reading from a monitor, chances are, you are most likely to be used to reading printed rather digital versions of your work.

Taps the syllables of the words as you read them. People tend to fail to detect their own errors, especially after writing. This is because people tend to remember and read based on their idea of what they wrote rather than the printed words, itself. The only way for you to check your work thoroughly is to tap each syllable and slowly check for errors as you read on.

Divide jobs into different steps. You can proofread for spelling errors first. Afterwards for punctuation usage, then for checking and verifying facts.

Double tap the ends of the words. Checking the endings of the words allows you to verify whether you have correctly used the words according to the number (i.e. whether plural or singular) or tense (whether past tense or not).

Circle punctuations in the end. This will help you verify your punctuations. Doing this after each sentence will also help you make sure you place periods after each of them.

Enlist the help of a software. There are a number of web-based grammar checkers that offer proofreading service for a price. If you are using MS Word, you can also enable its grammar checker functions to check for your grammar while you write. Be warned, however, of the limitations of machines. Still, nothing can beat the propensity and ability of a human mind when it comes to assessing and correcting a write-up.

Conclusion

You just finish a book filled with secrets on how to become an effective and successful copywriter. Your journey towards becoming a successful one will only start the moment you decide to become one.

You have been given tips and techniques on how to perform and perfect the craft. What remains now is for you to venture out and practice the craft.

Although it will certainly be hard for you for your first few weeks (or even months) rest assured that things get better with time and experience. Given with enough time, you will end up being one of the best (and most successful) copywriters.

Thank You Page

I want to personally thank you for reading my book. I hope you found information in this book useful and I would be very grateful if you could leave your honest review about this book. I certainly want to thank you in advance for doing this.

If you have the time, you can check my other books too.

www.ingramcontent.com/pod-product-compliance
Lightning Source LLC
LaVergne TN
LVHW021745060526
838200LV00052B/3480